CW01513015

Original title:

Labyrinth of Dreams

Author: Aron Pilviste

ISBN HARDBACK: 978 1 80560 989 6

ISBN PAPERBACK: 978-1-80561-550-7

The Ascent of the Veiled Mind

In shadows deep, the thoughts take flight,
A journey forged in the quiet night.
Whispers swirl, secrets intertwine,
Each step unfolds the veiled design.

Mountains rise, the path unclear,
Yet hope ignites within the sphere.
With every breath, a truth unwinds,
The ascent leads to the veiled mind.

Through fog and fear, courage transpires,
Igniting deep, forgotten fires.
Guided by stars, we seek the glow,
Unraveling the depths below.

Each thought a thread in fate's grand weave,
The tapestry reveals what we believe.
In silence vast, connections blend,
The veiled mind's journey will not end.

Reflections in the Misty Mirror

In the glass where silence dwells,
Images dance like whispered spells.
Misty contours reveal the past,
Each fleeting glance, a memory cast.

Eyes that search through veils of time,
Seeking truths in shadows prime.
In every ripple, stories plead,
Reflections guiding, hearts will lead.

Fragments born of dreams untold,
In silver light, the visions unfold.
Moments lost in fleeting grace,
Through misty mirrors, we find our place.

With every gaze, a layer lifts,
The soul unearths forgotten gifts.
In stillness deep, the echoes play,
Reflections In the mist won't sway.

Echoes of the Enchanted

In forests deep where whispers dwell,
Magic lingers, casting its spell.
Each rustling leaf, a tale retold,
Of wonders vast and dreams of old.

Through twilight shades, the shadows creep,
Awakening secrets that we keep.
Voices rise like songs of lore,
Echoes beckon from the forest floor.

In murmurs soft, the night ignites,
A dance of stars and phantom lights.
With every step, enchantments weave,
The echoes call us to believe.

Branches sway, a melody spins,
An orchestra of nature begins.
With hearts aligned to the ancient song,
In enchanted echoes, we belong.

The Timeless Exchange

In the hush of dawn, whispers blend,
Time unfolds, a circular end.
Each moment shared, a timeless flow,
In quiet grace, we come to know.

Words like petals drift and sway,
In the garden where thoughts play.
With every glance, horizons shift,
The timeless exchange, a precious gift.

Beneath the sun, shadows stretch long,
Unity found in a silent song.
With every heartbeat, life aligns,
The timeless dance of love defines.

As stars embrace the velvet night,
In dreams we find our shared insight.
The cosmos hums through space and time,
In the timeless exchange, we climb.

The Spiral Path to Nowhere

Winding paths of shadowed stone,
Lead to places we can't own.
Stepping softly, lost in thought,
Whispers of the past are caught.

Twisting turns and fading light,
Guide the heart through endless night.
With each step, the silence grows,
And questions linger, who still knows?

Beneath the trees, a secret sigh,
Where echoes of our dreams still lie.
In the labyrinth, truth is thin,
Finding peace where none has been.

Yet onward still, the journey goes,
Through tangled roots and thorny prose.
A spiral leads us round again,
Toward the start, but not the end.

Midnight's Tangle

Stars flicker softly in the haze,
Silver threads of whispered praise.
Underneath the moon's embrace,
Time weaves its delicate lace.

Shadows dance beneath the trees,
Carried on the midnight breeze.
Moving to a silent tune,
Where dreams are born beneath the moon.

Moments stretch and then they bend,
In a tangle without end.
Love and longing, chasing light,
Both entwined in endless night.

The heart beats in a rhythm rare,
Caught in dreams we choose to share.
As dawn approaches, fears arise,
Weaving tales of sweet goodbyes.

Dances in the Faded Hour

Twilight hushes, colors blend,
Time stretches, breathes, and bends.
In the dimming, shadows play,
As dusk invites the night to stay.

Graceful forms in softest glow,
Spin like leaves in autumn's flow.
Each step whispers tales of old,
In the quiet, dreams unfold.

Moments linger, softly spun,
Until the last of day is done.
In the silence, hearts ignite,
Dancing souls take up their flight.

With every twirl, a memory fades,
A fleeting touch through twilight shades.
In this faded hour, we find,
The beauty of a restless mind.

Illusions of the Mind's Eye

Mirrors shatter, truths distort,
Thoughts collide in whispered court.
Dancing shadows cast their spell,
In a world where phantoms dwell.

Fleeting moments blend and blur,
Waves of whispers start to stir.
In the depths where visions gleam,
Reality's a fractured dream.

Questions rise like smoke and flame,
Chasing echoes of a name.
What is real, what is disguise?
Chasing light, we seek the prize.

Through the maze of thoughts we tread,
Finding paths that call us dead.
Illusions dance, but we must see,
The truth lies in what will be.

Shadows of the Night

Whispers linger in the air,
Flickering lights hide in despair,
Darkness paints the silent ground,
In shadows deep, secrets are found.

Moonlight weaves through trembling trees,
Casting dreams upon the breeze,
Footsteps echo soft and low,
Guided by the stars' faint glow.

Night unfolds its velvet cloak,
As distant voices softly spoke,
In the hush, the world feels right,
Embraced by shadows of the night.

Glimmers dance on silver streams,
Carrying the weight of dreams,
With every hush, the heart takes flight,
Cradled in the arms of night.

As dawn breaks, shadows take their bow,
The night gives way, gentle and slow,
Yet in the light, the echoes stay,
Whispers of night guide the day.

Echoes of a Waking Mind

In the stillness, thoughts collide,
Dreams and reality, side by side,
A symphony of voices near,
Whispers of what we hold dear.

Morning light spills through the pane,
Awakens hope amidst the pain,
Fractured pieces start to blend,
In echoes, hearts begin to mend.

Each breath a canvas, wide and free,
Painting visions that yearn to be,
In the quiet, shadows fade,
As clarity begins to wade.

Time pauses in this sacred space,
Embracing thoughts, the mind's embrace,
From dusk to dawn, we seek and find,
Transcend the realms of the waking mind.

And as the world begins to spin,
The journey starts, the path within,
In each echo, a story unfolds,
Whispering truths that time holds.

Threads of the Unseen

Weave the fabric of the day,
In subtle hues, dreams softly play,
Invisible threads bind us tight,
In every moment, love ignites.

Gentle hands stitch hopes and fears,
Crafting visions through laughter and tears,
In shadows cast, we find our way,
Threads of the unseen lead our sway.

Through the tapestry of our mind,
Patterns emerge, so rare to find,
Silken whispers call our name,
In the quiet, none feel the same.

Every heartbeat, every sigh,
Connects us all as time goes by,
In the silence, stories weave,
Threads of the unseen, we believe.

As dawn dawns, we start anew,
With every thread, a brighter view,
Together, stitching life's grand design,
In woven paths, our souls entwine.

Through the Haze of Reverie

Drifting softly on whispered dreams,
Reality bends, or so it seems,
In the twilight where shadows play,
The heart dances, lost in sway.

Thoughts unfurl like morning mist,
In the haze, moments twist,
Echoes linger, sweet and light,
Through the haze of fading night.

Each sigh a step on pathways bright,
Guided by stars, soft and white,
In the stillness, visions bloom,
Finding peace in the quiet room.

With every heartbeat, time can pause,
In reverie, we find the cause,
To live and dream, to soar above,
Through the haze, we share our love.

As the day calls, we gently rise,
Carrying dreams beneath the skies,
In every layer, shadows weave,
Through the haze, we dare to believe.

Visions Carved in Ether

In dreams where shadows play,
The whispers drift and sway.
A canvas of the night,
With stars to guide our flight.

Veils of silk and time,
Unravel in soft rhyme.
Silhouettes softly weave,
As night begins to cleave.

Moments lost in air,
Dance lightly, unaware.
A breath of twilight's grace,
Each flicker leaves no trace.

In silence, visions blend,
Where every start can end.
The heart's ethereal glow,
Forever seeks to know.

Among the cosmic streams,
We chase our sweetest dreams.
In ether's gentle fold,
Every story's told.

Fantasies of Forgotten Streets

In alleys draped with vines,
Whispers cling to old signs.
Echoes of laughter drift,
Through shadows, tales uplift.

Cracked cobblestones below,
Reveal where memories flow.
Every window holds a gaze,
Locked in a time-worn haze.

Lanterns flicker with sighs,
As dusk begins to rise.
Footsteps whisper softly here,
In corners, secrets near.

The air rich with the past,
Where moments weave and cast.
Each heartbeat sings a song,
Of where we once belonged.

Yet time will not erase,
The warmth of each embrace.
These streets alive with dreams,
Hold more than what it seems.

Twisted Paths of Memory

Winding roads of thought,
In tangled webs we're caught.
Familiar scents ignite,
A journey lost to night.

Fragments of a smile,
Recall with every mile.
In corners of the mind,
A treasure we may find.

Faces drift like smoke,
In echoes soft they spoke.
Time's hands, they twist and turn,
In shadows where we yearn.

Held in a gentle gaze,
The past in gilded haze.
Memories softly plead,
To linger, to be freed.

Though time may pull apart,
The threads tie to the heart.
In labyrinths we roam,
We find each path a home.

Refractions of Dusk

Through prisms of the night,
Colors blend and take flight.
Each shimmer soft and rare,
A canvas of the air.

Shadows dance on the walls,
As twilight softly calls.
Textures of the fading light,
Weave magic into night.

In whispers of the breeze,
We seek the lost degrees.
With every breath we draw,
We witness nature's law.

The horizon bleeds and sways,
In the final gleaming rays.
Echoes of the day's last song,
In the dusk where we belong.

Reflections fade away,
As dreams begin to play.
In twilight's calm embrace,
We find our perfect space.

Dueling Realities

In shadows cast by flickering light,
Two worlds collide, an endless fight.
One whispers truth, the other lies,
As echoes dance beneath the skies.

The clock ticks loud, the air grows thin,
A battle raged both shy and thin.
What is the dream, and what is real?
Each moment shifts, it's hard to feel.

A glimpse of hope amid the strife,
In every choice, we shape our life.
The ties that bind, the threads that fray,
We forge our path, come what may.

In twilight's grasp, the truth unveils,
The heart's desire, the longing trails.
Two sides of fate forever dance,
In every breath, a fleeting chance.

So dare to leap, to take the ride,
Embrace the chaos, all inside.
For in this duel, we find our way,
In every night, awaits the day.

Mystical pathways of Nightfall

Beneath the stars where secrets dwell,
Mystical pathways weave a spell.
Whispers float on velvet air,
As dreams take flight, without a care.

The moonlight bathes the world in grace,
Shadows dance, a spectral race.
With every step, the heart ignites,
In night's embrace, the soul unites.

Ancient echoes softly call,
Through tangled woods, past twilight's thrall.
The fireflies glint, a guiding sign,
Hearts entwined in dreams divine.

A symphony of silence flows,
Revealing truths that night bestows.
The cosmos holds a whispered plea,
Join the dance, be wild and free.

In shadowed paths, let courage soar,
Discover realms you can explore.
For in the dark, a spark ignites,
As life transforms in starry nights.

The Unraveled Story

In pages worn, the tale unfolds,
Of whispered dreams and secrets told.
Each line is stitched with time and care,
A journey shared, a love laid bare.

Through tangled plots and twisting fates,
The heart beats loud, as tension waits.
Every character, a piece of truth,
A reflection of our shared youth.

The ink may fade, the words may blur,
Yet echoes linger, feelings stir.
With every chapter, life invites,
A dance of hopes, a clash of rights.

The ending's near, the climax nigh,
Yet in our hands, it's ours to try.
For every story finds its way,
In myriad forms, night into day.

With open hearts, the pages turn,
For in our souls, the lessons burn.
An unraveling of what we know,
In every ending, new seeds grow.

The Forgotten Corners of Sleep

In shadows deep, where dreams retreat,
Whispers linger, soft and sweet.
A world unfolds, so far away,
In slumber's arms, we long to stay.

Forgotten tales in quiet nights,
Bathed in the glow of moonlit sights.
Fleeting moments, drifting by,
Echoes soft as night birds sigh.

Ghostly figures, memories blend,
In twilight zones, where night won't end.
We chase the wisps, the fleeting gleam,
In the corners of our hidden dream.

Awakening calls, the dawn breaks through,
Yet still we hold to dreams so true.
For in the corners, treasures dwell,
In every sigh, a silent spell.

So lay your head, and drift away,
To those forgotten corners, stay.
Where time stands still, and shadows creep,
In the embrace of endless sleep.

Lost in the Shifting Sands

Underneath the blazing sun,
Footprints vanish, one by one.
Winds of change sweep through the land,
Whispers soft in shifting sand.

Mirages dance upon the dunes,
A symphony of ancient tunes.
Lost horizons, distant dreams,
Life is not quite what it seems.

Every grain tells a tale of old,
Secrets wrapped in suns of gold.
Time slips by in golden strands,
Caught between those shifting lands.

Stars appear as night descends,
Guiding seekers, where it bends.
Hope concealed in every swirl,
The heart's compass begins to whirl.

In this desert, find your grace,
Through the trials, it's a race.
For every step of earth you stand,
You're finding truth in shifting sand.

Secrets Beneath the Surface

Hidden deep where shadows dwell,
Beneath the waves, a silent shell.
Whispers echo from the deep,
In murky depths, secrets sleep.

Tales of love and loss abide,
In currents dark, where dreams confide.
Secrets swirl, like ocean's foam,
In the depths, we're never home.

Treasure lies in sunken ships,
With every dive, our heartbeat skips.
Journey down through water's veil,
Where every whisper tells a tale.

Bubbles rise, a silent song,
In the depths, where we belong.
Unlock the mysteries below,
In silence, let the secrets flow.

Surface tension breaks apart,
Bringing forth the hidden heart.
In liquid realms, we find release,
Hidden truths that bring us peace.

Twilight's Enigmatic Journey

As the sun dips low and light recedes,
Twilight weaves its mystic beads.
Colors blend in a soft embrace,
Time drifts in a slow-paced race.

A hush falls over the waking land,
Day's farewell with a gentle hand.
Silhouettes dance on the edge of sight,
In the shadows, dreams ignite.

Unraveling tales of the fading light,
The stars awaken, shimmering bright.
Pathways shift in the dimming glow,
Mysteries linger where few will go.

Each heartbeat echoes a whispered plea,
For the magic that twilight will see.
In twilight's grip, we lose our fears,
As night unveils the world's true mirrors.

So let the colors blend and merge,
In the twilight's calm, we emerge.
To journey forth where shadows twine,
In the enigmas, our spirits align.

Twilit Corridor

In shadows deep, where whispers dwell,
A path unfolds, a secret spell.
The twilight dances, soft and low,
In corridors where few dare go.

Ethereal light and echoes blend,
Each step a journey, a soul to mend.
Through realms of dusk, the heart takes flight,
In the embrace of fading light.

The walls hold stories, lost and found,
In every crack, in every sound.
Time bends softly, like a sigh,
As dreams and memories drift by.

A golden hue, a fleeting glance,
Invites the mind to dare a dance.
With silent steps on cobbled floor,
The twilight corridor opens its door.

In every corner, shadows creep,
While secrets, ancient, softly sleep.
A journey ends where it began,
In twilight's hush, the soul can span.

The Celestial Riddle

Stars align in a cosmic weave,
Each twinkle holds what we believe.
Galaxies spiral, secrets spun,
In the dance of dusk, we are one.

Questions float on silver streams,
What lies beyond our waking dreams?
In whispered winds, answers sway,
Guiding the lost along their way.

Nebulas blaze with colors bright,
Painting the canvas of the night.
Through endless voids, our spirits roam,
In search of truth, we find our home.

A riddle wrapped in twilight's glow,
In starlit paths, we learn to flow.
Beyond the veil, we reach and seek,
Discovering strength in every peak.

With every star and every sigh,
The celestial speaks, and we reply.
In the quiet of night, we find the key,
Unlocking the realms of mystery.

Walks Through the Uncharted

In lands unknown, where few have tread,
We set our course, following threads.
Each step a whisper, a call to roam,
In wild places, we find our home.

Mountains rise, majestic and grand,
Guardians shelter this untouched land.
With open hearts, we traverse the way,
Discovering wonders, come what may.

Rivers flow with secrets untold,
Echoes of stories waiting, bold.
Nature's canvas, a vibrant hue,
Reminds us all of dreams anew.

Through woods where sunlight rarely breaks,
Each rustle and call, the spirit wakes.
In jagged cliffs and valleys wide,
We forge our path, a timeless ride.

With every breath, we touch the skies,
In uncharted realms, our souls arise.
For in the journey, we come alive,
In wild embrace, our spirits thrive.

Dreams Adrift in Time

In twilight's grasp, where dreams do sail,
Memories linger, a wistful trail.
Time drifts softly on gentle waves,
Like whispered secrets in hidden caves.

Each moment holds a fragile thread,
Woven with wishes, unspoken dread.
In quiet hours, the heart confides,
As dreams adrift on time's great tides.

Faces float like clouds in the air,
Echoes of laughter, moments we share.
The past entwined with hopes to be,
In every glance, eternity.

A dance of shadows, a fleeting glance,
In silent yearning, we dare to dance.
With every heartbeat, we drift and sway,
In dreams adrift, we find our way.

With dawn's arrival, the dreams may fade,
But the memories linger, softly laid.
In every heartbeat, in every rhyme,
Our dreams remain, adrift in time.

Whispers Through the Maze

In a garden of twisting vines,
Secrets dance on the breeze,
Lost in paths where light entwines,
Footsteps fade, silence flees.

Whispers echo through the night,
Tales of dreams yet to unfold,
Guided by the moon's soft light,
Wonders waiting to be told.

Branches stretch like fingers wide,
Hiding stories, deep and old,
In the shadows, truth does hide,
Memories, bright and bold.

Each corner brings a new surprise,
Hope reflected in the dew,
With every turn, the heart will rise,
In the maze, we find what's true.

Shadows in the Night

Shadows creep in silence still,
The moon casts her gentle glow,
Whispers stir, against the chill,
As secrets from the darkness flow.

Stars twinkle high, a distant light,
Guiding hearts through dreams of flight,
In the depths where fears take flight,
Courage blooms, dispelling fright.

Through the haze, a figure gleams,
Laughter lingers in the air,
Chasing softly fading dreams,
In the night, we shed our care.

With each step, uncertainty,
Yet we wander, hand in hand,
For shadows hold infinity,
In the dark, love makes a stand.

Threads of the Forgotten

In the fabric of lost tales,
Threads of golden time unwind,
Whispers carried on the gales,
Fading echoes, intertwined.

Ancient voices softly call,
Beneath the weight of silent dreams,
Woven stories, large and small,
Flutter gently like moonbeams.

Each knot binds the past and now,
Stitching moments, clear and bright,
In the tapestry we vow,
To remember, hold the light.

As the twilight slowly fades,
Threads connect all that has been,
Carrying the hopes, cascades,
Of forgotten souls within.

Echoes of Slumbering Paths

In the quiet of the night,
Echoes of the past arise,
Wandering through dreams, a light,
Softly shining in our eyes.

Silent pathways twist and turn,
Mysteries tucked in the fog,
Lessons from the shadows learn,
As we journey through the log.

Whispers of the ages blend,
A gentle pull on hearts so true,
In our dreams, we will transcend,
Finding paths that lead to you.

Through the darkness, hope ignites,
Mapping out the way ahead,
With each step, our spirit fights,
In the echoes, dreams are fed.

Mosaics of the Subconscious

Fragments of thought scatter like light,
Patterns emerge in the quiet night.
Shadows whisper secrets untold,
In the depths where dreams unfold.

Colors blend in a tapestry vast,
Moments linger, memories cast.
Each piece a story waiting to shine,
Together they form a intricate design.

Beneath the surface, emotions swirl,
Hidden depths in a chaotic whirl.
Reflections of life, both bitter and sweet,
In this mosaic, fragments compete.

A dance of the mind in a silent space,
Searching for meaning in each trace.
Harmony rises from discordant tones,
In the subconscious, the heart finds its homes.

With every glance, new worlds appear,
A kaleidoscope of hope and fear.
Mosaics of whispers, delicate and bold,
In the silence, the truth is told.

The Veiled Passageways

Lost in corridors wrapped in mist,
Wonders await in the gentle twist.
Torches flicker with secrets bright,
Guiding footsteps through the night.

Doors of dreams stand ajar,
Inviting souls from near and far.
With each turn, a tale renews,
In these hallways, paths infuse.

Echoes linger in the still air,
Voices of those who once were there.
Shapes dancing in shadows cast,
Memories shimmering, fading fast.

Clarity hides in the labyrinth's core,
Each passage whispers of ancient lore.
With fear and courage, hearts will choose,
To wander onward, to win or lose.

Veils may shroud the ultimate truth,
Yet every step unveils our youth.
In the depths, courage must play,
Unlocking the veiled passageways.

Echoes of a Fading Echo

In the canyon where silence breathes,
Whispers linger like fallen leaves.
A voice once loud now soft and thin,
Echoes dart where shadows begin.

Time cascades in a gentle stream,
Memories flicker, fading gleam.
Each sound a ghost, a tale untold,
In the quiet, the past unfolds.

What was vibrant is now a sigh,
A distant call as moments fly.
Chasing echoes through the air,
Finding fragments everywhere.

Yet even as the echoes wane,
Their resonance will still remain.
Fleeting, they dance on the edge of night,
Reflections woven in fading light.

A song of sorrow, a balm of grace,
Captured in time, we still embrace.
In echoes of a fading echo we find,
The heart's soft rhythm, forever entwined.

Whispers in the Maze

Hidden pathways twist and turn,
Secrets linger, mysteries burn.
In this labyrinth, shadows play,
Whispers echoing, leading astray.

Each step taken, a choice made,
Between the bright and the deep shade.
Voices murmur just out of sight,
Drawing the heart toward the night.

Mirrors reflect with intent unclear,
Showing faces we hold dear.
Yet the maze offers layers of fate,
In whispers, the truths await.

Each corner turned reveals anew,
A dance of light, a shade of blue.
Guided by whispers, we carry on,
Towards the dawn, far from the darkened yawn.

In chaos lies a sacred space,
Where every maze finds its grace.
With open hearts, we'll seek and trace,
The whispers within the timeless maze.

Paths of Illusion

In shadows dance the dreams we chase,
With whispered hopes that time can't trace.
Each step a choice, a winding way,
Lost in the night, we dream of day.

Figures flicker at the edge of sight,
Guiding through the velvet night.
Yet paths diverge, and choices bind,
In this maze, the truth we find.

Mirrors shatter, reflections fade,
Moments linger where fears are laid.
Threads of fate weave in and out,
Lost in thoughts, we twist about.

A compass broken, stars align,
In every heart a secret sign.
We wander on, seeking our creed,
Through tangled paths, we're lost indeed.

The Enigma of Sleep

In twilight's hush, the world falls still,
Whispers weave their gentle thrill.
Dreams unfurl in a velvet sweep,
Caught in the enigma of sleep.

Stars are stories yet untold,
Shadows shimmer, bright and bold.
In slumber's grasp, we softly weave,
Entranced by what we dare believe.

Time collapses, moments bend,
Where waking thoughts and visions blend.
A fleeting glance at what could be,
In the realm of mystery.

Lost in layers of soft white mist,
Reality and dreams coexist.
The heartbeats echo, soft and deep,
In the wondrous world of sleep.

Echoing Hallways of the Heart

In corridors of tender light,
Echoes of laughter, hearts take flight.
Memories linger on the walls,
Whispers susurrate as twilight calls.

Each step resounds with hope and pain,
In these hallways, love's refrain.
Where every heartbeat finds a song,
United dreams where we belong.

Footprints trace the paths once walked,
In silent spaces, where we talked.
A symphony of all that's lost,
In quiet chambers, we pay the cost.

Time weaves tales with every breath,
In sacred spaces, love finds depth.
Through echoing hallways, we shall roam,
In the heart's embrace, we find our home.

Staircases to Nowhere

Amidst the fog, the stairs ascend,
Winding pathways that never end.
Each step a dream, a hope to find,
Yet leading nowhere, intertwined.

Caught in the loops of time and space,
A journey slow, a haunting grace.
Infinite climbs, yet still we strive,
Chasing echoes, feeling alive.

Hands reach out to grasp the air,
Invisible threads that lead to despair.
Faces wane like a distant star,
As we climb higher, yet fall afar.

The view from the top reveals the truth,
Fleeting moments, lost in youth.
With every step, a longing grows,
On staircases where no one knows.

The Gossamer Trail

A shimmer weaves through morning dew,
Soft whispers glide 'neath skies so blue.
Each step we take, the world will bloom,
In gossamer light, banishing gloom.

Upon this path, we dare to roam,
Chasing dreams that feel like home.
With every breath, a story unfolds,
In the warmth of sun, our hearts are bold.

Yet shadows linger, fleeting and slight,
Casting tales of the coming night.
The trail may fade, yet we will chase,
The beauty of life, in every space.

And as we walk with weary feet,
The gossamer threads of fate we meet.
In fragile strands, connections made,
A journey penned, never to fade.

The Maze of Echoing Silences

In whispered halls where shadows creep,
Echoes linger, secrets deep.
Every corner hides a breath,
In silence, we confront our death.

Walls of stone, a winding fate,
In stillness, we contemplate.
Time stands still, a ghostly dance,
Lost in thought, caught in a trance.

Yet through the maze, we find our way,
Guided by the light of day.
Each silence speaks a truth untold,
In echoes past, the future's gold.

And if we listen, hearts ajar,
The whispers lead us, near and far.
In this maze, we come alive,
Through echoes, we will always strive.

Spinning Threads of Thought

In quiet hours, my mind will weave,
A tapestry, the heart believes.
Threads of color, bright and bold,
Stories waiting to be told.

Each thought a strand in gentle hands,
Woven tightly, as life demands.
In twilight glow, ideas flow,
Intertwining, ebb and glow.

The loom vibrates with every spark,
A dance of dreams within the dark.
Through these threads, I find my voice,
In the fabric of fate, I rejoice.

With every twist, a new refrain,
Threads of sorrow, joy, and pain.
A journey crafted, piece by piece,
In the weaving, I find my peace.

Fables of the Nocturnal Traveler

Underneath the silver moon,
Whispers echo, night's sweet tune.
In shadows, secrets softly sigh,
The nocturnal traveler wanders by.

With every step, a story calls,
Through darkened woods and ancient halls.
In timeworn tales, the wild things play,
Fables carved by the light of day.

Stars above like lanterns gleam,
Guiding dreams through the twilight seam.
In whispered winds, the legends rise,
A world unseen before our eyes.

And in this fable, we find delight,
In the embrace of the velvet night.
For every traveler finds their truth,
In the timeless dance of forgotten youth.

Mysteries Woven in Moonlight

Beneath the silver glow, shadows dance,
Whispers of secrets, in twilight's trance.
Stars twinkle softly, hidden from sight,
Stories entwined in the arms of night.

The winds carry tales from distant lands,
Silhouettes linger in the moon's gentle hands.
Each moment a puzzle, frail and slight,
Mysteries woven in the fabric of night.

Forgotten echoes, a nocturnal song,
Guiding lost souls where they belong.
Every heartbeat pulses with light,
Hope and wonder twinkle, shining bright.

In the silence, dreams begin to soar,
Awakening magic we can't ignore.
A world of enchantment, holding tight,
Mysteries woven, everything feels right.

As dawn approaches, shadows take flight,
Yet memories linger, soft and light.
With the rising sun, we take our plight,
To chase the mysteries woven in night.

Fragments of a Shattered Reverie

Scattered pieces of dreams unfulfilled,
Echoes of laughter, hearts distanced, chilled.
In the corners of time, memories hide,
Fragments of moments, lost in the tide.

A clock ticks softly, marking the pain,
Faded reflections dance in the rain.
Shadows and light in a delicate fight,
Fragments collide, merging day and night.

Every sigh carries a silent plea,
Wishing for solace, yearning to be free.
Faces of strangers passing in flight,
Fragments of a past, just out of sight.

Winds whisper secrets; the heartbeats race,
In the silence lingers a forgotten grace.
Time's cruel hands steal away the light,
Fragments of sorrow blend with delight.

But in the stillness, hope starts to bloom,
With every sunset, there brightens a room.
A tapestry woven from pain and from fright,
Fragments assemble, aiming for light.

The Hidden Doorway

In the forest deep, where shadows weave,
A doorway awaits for those who believe.
Overgrown vines and forgotten trails,
Whispers of magic dance in the gales.

Step through the silence, a world anew,
Colors explode in every hue.
Beyond the threshold, dreams ignite,
The hidden doorway beckons in the night.

Time stands still in this sacred space,
Echoes of laughter fill the place.
Journey within, let your spirit take flight,
The hidden doorway reveals pure light.

With every heartbeat, the wonders unfold,
Stories of courage, tales of old.
In the heart of the woods, the stars shine bright,
Through the hidden doorway, darkness takes flight.

So wander the paths where few have roamed,
In search of the mysteries, we find our home.
For life is a journey of love and delight,
Through the hidden doorway, we find our light.

Mists of Forgotten Dreams

In the morning mist, shadows arise,
Faint echoes of laughter, lost in the skies.
Whispers of wishes that lingered too long,
Mists of forgotten dreams, bittersweet song.

Through veils of fog, the visions unfold,
Stories untold, waiting to be bold.
Each breath a memory, fading from sight,
Mists of forgotten dreams, lost in the night.

Time drips like dew on the petals rare,
Beauty entwined with a trace of despair.
Threads of the past in a delicate fight,
Mists of forgotten dreams, cloaked in the light.

Yet within the haze, hope starts to gleam,
In the quiet stillness, we dare to dream.
With courage we gather, taking our flight,
Through the mists of forgotten dreams, we ignite.

For every dawn breaks, shedding the night,
Rekindling visions, setting them right.
In the heart of the fog, love shines so bright,
Mists of forgotten dreams, guiding our sight.

Dreamscapes Entwined

In twilight's hush we gently tread,
Where whispers of the stars are spread.
A tapestry of visions bright,
We drift through realms of silver light.

Soft echoes call from distant days,
In swirling mists of emerald haze.
Together in this dreamlike game,
Our hearts ignite with passion's flame.

With every breath, new worlds unfold,
In vibrant hues of blue and gold.
We dance on clouds, both free and wild,
In this enchanted space, beguiled.

The nightingale sings sweet refrains,
While moonlit paths reveal our gains.
Each shadow casts a tale untold,
In realms where fear can't take its hold.

As dawn approaches, dreams must fade,
Yet in our hearts, their hues cascade.
For every night brings forth a chance,
To weave new dreams in endless dance.

Mirage of the Mind's Eye

In reflections of the mind's deep sea,
A mirage dances, wild and free.
Colors swirl in a boundless flight,
Illusions flicker, shadows ignite.

With every thought, new worlds arise,
Chasing visions in the skies.
The heartbeat of a dream unknown,
Echoes softly, we are not alone.

Waves of doubts crash on the shore,
Yet hope's light shines forevermore.
A labyrinth of thoughts we seek,
Voices whisper, tender and meek.

In corridors where silence creeps,
The mind unveils what the soul keeps.
Every corner, a unique sight,
Illumined by a hidden light.

As thoughts converge like stars at night,
A canvas glows with purest light.
Embrace the magic of the dream,
For all is not as it may seem.

Flickering Lanterns in the Dark

In shadows deep, where silence dwells,
Flickering lanterns cast their spells.
They guide the lost with gentle glow,
Through winding paths, where few dare go.

Each flame a tale, a timeless song,
Whispering secrets, deep and strong.
They dance in rhythms, soft and sweet,
A soothing balm for weary feet.

With every spark, new journeys start,
Illuminating the wandering heart.
A beacon's hope, through thick and thin,
A reminder that light grows from within.

Beyond the veil of dusk and pain,
Where dreams reside, and hope's refrain.
We gather strength from flickering beams,
In the night's embrace, we find our dreams.

So let us walk where shadows play,
With lanterns bright to show the way.
Together through the darkest hours,
We'll find our strength, like blooming flowers.

A Journey Beyond the Veil

Through whispered winds, we cross the veil,
Where echoes of the past prevail.
In twilight's grace, we dare to roam,
Finding solace far from home.

Winding paths of ancient stone,
In every heart, seeds of earth are sown.
Secrets flicker like fireflies,
Beneath the vast and starry skies.

In realms where shadows intertwine,
We seek the truth, both yours and mine.
Fragments of dreams, now intertwined,
A tapestry of souls enshrined.

As we embark on this unknown quest,
With open hearts, we face the test.
For every step draws us more near,
To wisdom forged from joy and fear.

Embracing all that life imparts,
The journey binds our restless hearts.
Together we shall come alive,
Beyond the veil, our spirits thrive.

The Infinite Thread

In shadows deep, the thread does weave,
Connecting hearts that dare believe.
A whisper floats through time and space,
Bound by love, we find our grace.

Each stitch a tale, both old and new,
Worn ribbons show the paths we drew.
With every knot, a story sewn,
In sacred bonds, we are not alone.

The loom of fate, a gentle guide,
Where dreams are spun, and hopes abide.
In every tear, in every cheer,
The tapestry of life appears.

Through tangled threads, we seek our way,
Beneath the stars, we long to stay.
With open hearts and hands so wide,
We treasure all, and love our ride.

When time unravels, still we hold,
The threads of warmth against the cold.
In woven paths, we dance and find,
The infinite thread that binds mankind.

Portals of the Sleeping Soul

In twilight's hush, the portals gleam,
Where dreams unfold like whispered themes.
A gentle sigh calls forth the night,
To cradle souls in soft twilight.

Through velvet veils, our spirits soar,
To realms unknown, we long for more.
In slumber deep, the shadows blend,
With echoes of a timeless friend.

Moonlit paths guide every heart,
To find the echoes, never part.
In realms of light, where silence reigns,
The sleeping soul, through joy, through pains.

Whispers linger in the air,
A sacred dance, a love affair.
With every breath, in dreams we chase,
The portals of an endless space.

Awake we rise, yet still we feel,
The tender ties, a woven reel.
In every dream, in every sigh,
The portals beckon, never shy.

A Journey Beyond the Veil

In twilight's grasp, a journey starts,
To cross the veil that life imparts.
With every step, the unknown calls,
In silent whispers, past time falls.

Through realms of shadow, light does gleam,
Beyond the edge of every dream.
A tapestry of souls entwined,
In cosmic dance, our fates aligned.

With eager hearts and open minds,
We seek the truth, where hope unwinds.
With courage warm, we tread the line,
Where worlds collide, and stars align.

Each heartbeat echoes in the void,
A symphony of love deployed.
Through every challenge, every fear,
We find the path that draws us near.

In twilight's arms, we stand as one,
Resilience born when day is done.
A journey vast, yet close we dwell,
In every heart, beyond the veil.

The Secret Dance of Night

Beneath the stars, the night unfolds,
A secret dance that time beholds.
In whispers soft, the shadows sway,
In graceful arcs, they fade away.

With every flicker, dreams ignite,
The moonlight casts its silver light.
Through winding paths where spirits roam,
The heartbeat of the night feels home.

In quiet corners, secrets dwell,
In every glance, a tale to tell.
The silence sings, we listen close,
As darkened skies begin to doze.

Stars twinkle bright, like distant chimes,
A melody that stirs through times.
With whispered sighs, the night draws near,
The secret dance of love sincere.

In twilight's arms, we spin and weave,
Embracing the magic we believe.
With every breath, the night enchants,
In softest rhythms, our spirit dances.

The Enchanted Dusk

As twilight drapes its silken cloak,
Whispers of dreams begin to weave.
Stars awaken from shadows spoke,
In colors that the heart believes.

The breeze carries a soft refrain,
A melody of the night's embrace.
Moonlight dances on silvery rain,
Painting shadows with gentle grace.

Creatures stir in the hush of eve,
Secret worlds emerge from the dark.
In the stillness, we dare to believe,
In the spark of a distant spark.

The horizon flickers, a fiery hue,
Guiding the lost with ethereal light.
Each heartbeat echoes the magic anew,
Binding the day with the mysteries of night.

So let us wander where dreams take flight,
Under the spell of the enchanting dusk.
In every shadow a story ignites,
In every sigh, whispers of trust.

Patterns of the Unseen

Tangled threads of fate interlace,
In colors that flicker and flare.
Beyond the veil we seek to trace,
The patterns suspended in air.

Each heartbeat a pulse, each thought a line,
Woven in silence, a tapestry grows.
Shadows that dance in a rhythm divine,
Hold secrets that only the brave can know.

Ripples spread in the still of the night,
Each wave is a whisper of dreams yet to be.
The fabric reveals both darkness and light,
Connecting the hearts of you and me.

Beneath the surface, stories abound,
Hidden depths that invite us to see.
In the uncharted, we lose and we found,
The intricacies of what we can be.

So let us explore these unseen patterns,
In every moment, a chance to unfold.
Mapped by the stars and the dreams we gather,
Our destinies written in threads of gold.

The Hidden Gates of Fantasy

Beneath the arches of an ancient tree,
Lies a door that whispers our names.
Through creaking hinges, we long to see,
The realm where magic forever claims.

In gardens where wildflowers bloom,
Each petal holds tales of forgotten lore.
Their fragrance lifts us beyond the gloom,
To lands where wonder opens every door.

Clouds become castles, the sky a sea,
Dragons dance in a shimmering haze.
With every heartbeat, we are set free,
In the corridors of endless gaze.

The hidden gates swing open with grace,
Inviting those who dare to believe.
To wander the realms where dreams interlace,
And in the unknown, we learn to weave.

So take my hand, let us step inside,
To a world where stories are spun.
In the heart of the fantasy, we abide,
Where every ending is just begun.

Wandering in the Nebula

In the embrace of the vast unknown,
Stars are born in a cosmic dance.
Galaxies shimmer and brightly shone,
Inviting all to take a chance.

Drifting through the colors unfurled,
The fabric of time weaves in waves.
Whispers of futures, dreams of worlds,
In stardust paths, the heart braves.

Nebulas swirl with a vibrant glow,
Carving stories in the velvet night.
In stillness, secrets begin to flow,
As we chase shadows, lost in light.

A compass guided by glints and gleams,
Each heartbeat merges with cosmic time.
Lost in the beauty of boundless dreams,
A journey beyond reason and rhyme.

So let us wander through endless skies,
In the heart of the nebula, bold and free.
Where the universe opens, and wonder flies,
Painting our spirits in eternity.

Veils of Ethereal Night

In shadows deep the secrets lie,
Draped in stars, they softly sigh.
Whispers weave through moonlit threads,
In the stillness, silence spreads.

A tapestry of dreams unwind,
Casting visions, free the mind.
Through the darkness, colors bloom,
Veils of night, dispel the gloom.

Eclipsed by time, the moments freeze,
Fleeting glimpses carried by breeze.
Veils of dreams, they rise and fall,
In the night, we hear their call.

Beneath the glow of silver light,
Spirits dance, embracing flight.
In the quiet, magic flows,
Veils of night, where wonder grows.

Embrace the peace, let go of fear,
In the velvet dusk, draw near.
For within these veils, we find,
The secrets of the heart and mind.

The Withering Path of Whispers

Along the road where shadows dwell,
A tale of sorrow, lost to tell.
Echoes of laughter fade to cries,
The withering path beneath our skies.

Softly spoken, secrets shared,
In the thorns, hearts have bared.
Memories linger, sweet and sour,
Fading light, a wilting flower.

Leaves once vibrant, now a shade,
The price of love in silence paid.
Whispers trace where hope has flown,
In the stillness, pain has grown.

Through tangled roots, our fears ensnare,
Longing hearts in silent prayer.
For every step, a ghostly plea,
On this path, we yearn to be free.

Yet within the dusk, a flicker glows,
A promise in the dark, hope grows.
Follow whispers, seek the light,
On the withering path of night.

Tides of the Unconscious Sea

In the depths where dreams reside,
Tides are shifting, love and pride.
A journey through the ebb and flow,
Of hidden thoughts we dared not show.

Waves of whispers crash and crest,
Cleansing souls, a timeless quest.
In the calm, we hear the call,
Of the sea, embracing all.

Thoughts like currents, swift and bold,
Unfurl the stories yet untold.
With each pulse, emotions sway,
In the depths, we drift away.

Moonlit ripples, glimmer bright,
Guiding us through the quiet night.
Lost in visions, wide and free,
Tides of our unconscious sea.

As we navigate the vast unknown,
In the ocean, seeds are sown.
Through the storm, we'll find our way,
Embrace the tides of night and day.

The Lurking Presence

In the corner of my eye, it stirs,
A whisper soft, the silence purrs.
Shapes that tremble, shadows creep,
The lurking presence haunts my sleep.

In the darkness, fear takes flight,
A ghostly figure in the night.
Fingers trace upon the wall,
A hidden truth, a silent call.

With every breath, the tension grows,
A stirring dread that nobody knows.
Through the quiet, footsteps sound,
The lurking presence all around.

Time stands still, the world a blur,
An unseen force begins to stir.
In the stillness, something waits,
The lurking presence, twisting fates.

Yet in the shadows, light may break,
A chance to rise, a chance to wake.
Facing fears, we learn to see,
The lurking presence sets us free.

Secrets of the Phantasmagoria

In whispers dark, the shadows dance,
With secrets cloaked in a fleeting glance.
Mystery thrives where illusions ignite,
Revealing truths in the blackest night.

Figures twist in the twilight haze,
Lost in a labyrinth of ethereal ways.
Echoes of dreams, they rise and fall,
Painting the silence, captivating all.

Fleeting visions, like smoke in the air,
Drift through the mind, elusive and rare.
Each flicker bright, then fading away,
In the phantasmagoria where phantoms play.

The heart knows tales of shadows and light,
Whispering secrets in the depth of night.
In this mystic world, we find our place,
In the embrace of an enigmatic grace.

So dare to venture, hold tight your dream,
For life is more than it may seem.
Embrace the unknown, let it unfold,
In the secrets of life, let your story be told.

Shadows Along the Glistening Path

Beneath the stars, shadows weave,
Along the path, dreams believe.
Glistening lights dance on the ground,
Whispers of magic, all around.

Each step taken, a story spun,
In the glow of the moon, we run.
Echoes of laughter, soft and light,
Guiding our hearts through the deepening night.

Branches sway, like thoughts on breeze,
Carrying secrets among the trees.
A moment captured, fleeting and bright,
Shadows embrace, holding us tight.

As the journey unfolds with grace,
We glimpse the wonders in this space.
In glimmering dreams, we find our fate,
Shadows along the path resonate.

So keep your eyes to the skies so vast,
For each shadow leads us, unsurpassed.
With every stride on this vibrant way,
We dance with shadows, come what may.

Enigma in the Ether

In twilight's hush, the ether glows,
Weaving enigmas, concealed in throes.
A realm of secrets, undefined,
Where whispers linger, and truths unwind.

Veils of mist enshroud the night,
Cradling wonders just out of sight.
In the stillness, echoes call,
The enigma beckons, captivating all.

Stars collide in luminous play,
Painting the cosmos in shades of gray.
In the silence, a story unfolds,
In every heartbeat, the mystery molds.

Fleeting visions drift through time's mirage,
As heartbeats dance in a quiet barrage.
In the ether, a magic lies,
Where enigmas linger, and the spirit flies.

So wander freely through this dream,
In the world of ether, more than it seems.
Embrace the shadows, the light above,
For the enigma whispers of boundless love.

A Journey Through Flickering Lights

In the dusk, where shadows play,
Flickering lights guide our way.
Each glow a beacon, soft and bright,
Leading us through the tender night.

Moments twinkle, like stars anew,
Illuminating paths we pursue.
With every step, dreams come to life,
A journey blooms, in the heart of strife.

Whispers of magic, in every glance,
In the dance of light, we find our chance.
Guided by hope, we brave the dark,
With flickering lights igniting the spark.

As the world turns, we spiral on,
Through the flickers, till the dawn.
With each heartbeat, the story flows,
In the warmth of light, the spirit grows.

So take my hand, and journey near,
Through shadows bright, we have no fear.
In this tapestry, we intertwine,
In flickering lights, your heart meets mine.

The Enchanted Passageway

Through ivy leaves the secrets hide,
A winding path where whispers bide.
Golden light begins to dance,
In this realm, you take a chance.

Footsteps echo soft and low,
Guiding hearts where lovers go.
Ancient trees with stories old,
Guard the dreams that time unfolds.

Moonlight spills onto the ground,
Magic swirls in night profound.
A hidden door to worlds anew,
Awaiting those who dare pursue.

Glimmers spark and visions gleam,
In this place, you'll find your dream.
A passage through the veil of night,
Leading souls to realms of light.

Fables of the Dreamweaver

In a realm where dreams collide,
The Dreamweaver begins to guide.
Threads of silver, soft and bright,
Weaving tales of starry night.

Whispers dance upon the breeze,
Tales of love and mysteries.
In the hush of twilight's grace,
Stories bloom in time and space.

Scarlet threads of joy entwine,
Golden seams of fate align.
Every sigh and every tear,
Stitched together, crystal clear.

From these fables, hope will rise,
Birthing visions in the skies.
With each tale, new worlds are spun,
In dreams, we are forever one.

Enigmas Beneath the Surface

Ripples dance on tranquil lakes,
Beneath the shade, the stillness wakes.
Mysteries lie within the deep,
Secrets only silence keeps.

Glimmers hide in waters clear,
Echoes whisper, soft yet near.
What lies beneath the quiet flow,
A realm where few have dared to go?

Fishes glint like scattered stars,
Among the reeds, the silence jars.
Each murmur speaks of tales untold,
Of treasures lost and dreams of gold.

Dive beneath and feel the chill,
Embrace the truth, the heart's sweet thrill.
Within the depths, find what you seek,
Enigmas wait for hearts that speak.

Reflections Among the Shadows

In twilight's grasp, the shadows play,
Whispers fade at end of day.
Mirrored light and dark unite,
Where silence breathes and dreams take flight.

Faces drift like passing clouds,
In the dusk, the heart enshrouds.
Reflections dance on cobblestone,
Echoes linger, softly moan.

Through the veil of dusk and dawn,
Lost in thoughts that ponder on.
Each whisper holds a tale to share,
In shadows deep, we find our care.

Glimmers spark in fleeting sight,
In fading dusk, we chase the light.
Among the shadows, truths reside,
In quiet dreams, our hopes abide.

The Infinite Winding

In valleys deep, where echoes fade,
A path unwinds, in twilight's shade.
With every step, the shadows blend,
A journey lost, where dreams transcend.

The winding road, a silent plea,
Whispers secrets, wild and free.
Around the bend, the stars ignite,
Guided by an unseen light.

In murmurings of ancient trees,
The tales of time ride on the breeze.
In every turn, a world anew,
In curiosity, I wander through.

The endless maze, a canvas drawn,
With colors rich, of dusk and dawn.
Each winding thought flows like a stream,
A tapestry woven from a dream.

And so I walk, through night and day,
An infinite winding, come what may.
In every heartbeat, in every sigh,
I find the path that will not die.

Gossamer Treads

On fragile threads, the morning weaves,
A tapestry of hope, believe.
With gentle hands, the sun aligns,
To bring forth life in soft designs.

Through dewdrops bright, the dawn will sing,
Of whispers sweet, and fragile things.
A dance of light, a fleeting grace,
In every moment, magic's trace.

With every step, the gossamer glows,
In silver beams, as the cool wind blows.
Through fields of dreams, our shadows play,
In the soft embrace of a waking day.

Each tread I take, a wish, a prayer,
In this delicate world, so rare.
The gossamer speaks, though unseen it seems,
Of love and hope and tender dreams.

And as we wander, hand in hand,
We'll weave together, a lasting strand.
In gossamer threads, our lives entwined,
In every heartbeat, joy defined.

Chasing Phantoms in Reverie

In twilight's grasp, the phantoms roam,
Among the shades, they find their home.
With whispered secrets, they softly glide,
In realms of dreams, they bide their time.

Through misty halls where shadows play,
In silent echoes, night turns to day.
I chase their forms through the dusky veil,
As visions flicker, a haunting trail.

With every step, their laughter fades,
In fleeting glances, life cascades.
I reach for light, a spark divine,
Yet they dissolve with the sands of time.

In reverie's depths, the phantoms twirl,
Invoking peace in a dreamlike whirl.
A labyrinth of thoughts, so deep and bright,
Where shadows blend with the lingering light.

And as I wander through this night,
I find my heart in shadows' flight.
Chasing phantoms, I learn to see,
In every moment, what's meant to be.

The Twisted Corridors of Night

In corridors dark, where silence creeps,
The night unfolds, its secrets deep.
With twisted turns and shadows long,
The heart of darkness sings its song.

Through every corner, whispers call,
In this realm, I feel so small.
Each heartbeat echoes, soft and low,
As mysteries start to ebb and flow.

Where candles flicker, the shadows dance,
In every glimmer, a hidden chance.
I walk the line 'tween fear and grace,
In the corridors, I find my place.

With every sigh, the night concedes,
To thoughts that wander, as my heart bleeds.
In twisted paths, the truth entwines,
A thread of fate that brightly shines.

And as I tread through darkly light,
I learn to trust the power of night.
For in these corridors, I am free,
To chase the dreams that live in me.

The Tapestry of Lost Wishes

In the fabric of dreams, they weave,
Threads of hope, we yearn to believe.
Faded colors, stories once bright,
Whispers of wishes, lost in the night.

Each stitch a memory, caught in the seams,
A reminder of laughter, and childhood dreams.
Yet time unravels, the fibers grow thin,
In the tapestry's heart, we find what's akin.

Silken desires, scattered like dust,
Fragile and fleeting, they vanish, they rust.
With every pull, the pattern does shift,
A portrait of longing, a bittersweet gift.

Beneath the moon's gaze, they shimmer and fade,
Echoes of wishes, in shadows they wade.
An intricate dance of what could have been,
In the depths of the night, they softly spin.

Yet still, we gather the threads that remain,
We stitch them together, despite the pain.
For in every loss, a new hope may rise,
The tapestry glows with bright, starry skies.

Navigating Through Starlit Corridors

In corridors paved with silver light,
We wander through dreams, dances of night.
Each turn a voyage, each step a song,
Guided by stars, where we truly belong.

Whispers of galaxies, secrets untold,
Stories of ancients, in starlight unfold.
With every heartbeat, the universe hums,
Echoes of past, in the silence it drums.

Celestial pathways, infinite glow,
We chase the comets, let our spirits flow.
In the dark corners, where shadows collide,
We find our truths, and in wonder, abide.

Yet time stands still in this vast cosmic sea,
The mysteries beckon, a call to be free.
Navigating dreams, with hope as our guide,
Through starlit corridors, where dreams reside.

With every starlight, new visions take flight,
We dance through the cosmos, in pure delight.
Embracing the wonders, the beauty, the grace,
In this tapestry woven, we each find our place.

Reverberations of Slumber's Embrace

In slumber's embrace, we drift and we sway,
Dreams like soft waves, carry us away.
Echoes of whispers, the night softly calls,
In the depths of darkness, our spirit enthralls.

Moonlight cascades, a gentle caress,
Wrapping us sweetly in tranquility's dress.
As shadows dance lightly, fleeting and brief,
We're cradled by visions, not bound by belief.

In this quiet realm, where silence unfolds,
Our fears and our joys are tenderly told.
With every heartbeat, the night sings a tune,
A lullaby woven by stars and the moon.

Dreams weave their magic, a tapestry fine,
Finding our solace, the stars realign.
As reverberations of slumber entwine,
We awaken anew, like tea steeped in time.

With dawn on the horizon, dreams start to fade,
Yet whispers remain, a sweet serenade.
In the stillness of morning, we carry the grace,
Of slumber's embrace, in the heart, leaves its trace.

Echoing Footsteps in Mist

In the still of the night, footsteps softly tread,
Through the whispers of mist, where secrets are fed.
Each step a soft echo, a story unspun,
In the dance of the shadows, where memories run.

Underneath the cloak of the moon's gentle light,
Figures appear, then dissolve into night.
An ethereal journey, through fog and through fear,
Treading the line between far and near.

With every soft murmur, the past lingers on,
In the echoes of footsteps, where dreams have been drawn.
The mist wraps around, like a lover once known,
In the silence of twilight, we're never alone.

Through the haze of the evening, we wander and sigh,
Chasing the whispers of days that went by.
In the dance of the twilight, the heart starts to yearn,
For the echoes of moments we hope to return.

Yet with every step forward, we leave parts behind,
In the fog of remembrance, we seek and we find.
Echoing footsteps, in the mist we embrace,
A journey through time, in this timeless space.

www.ingramcontent.com/pod-product-compliance
Ingram Content Group UK Ltd.
Pitfield, Milton Keynes, MK11 3LW, UK
UKHW021441280125
4335UKWH00035B/335